DATE DUE

FEB 0 1 2000	
MAR 0 9 2000	
MAY 0 5 2000	
JUL 2 9 2000	
SEP 1 8 2000	
JUL 0 3 2001	
JUL 1 2 2001	
6-27	

Robert Louis Stevenson

My Shadow

illustrated by Ted Rand

G. P. PUTNAM'S SONS • NEW YORK

G. P. Putnam's Sons, a division of The Putnam & Grosset Book Group,
200 Madison Avenue, New York, NY 10016
Published simultaneously in Canada
Printed in Hong Kong by South China Printing Co. (1988) Ltd.
Type design by Golda Laurens

Library of Congress Cataloging-in-Publication Data
Stevenson, Robert Louis, 1850–1894. My shadow.
Summary: An illustrated version of the poem in which
a child describes her relationship with her shadow.
1. Shades and shadows—Juvenile poetry.
2. Children's poetry, Scottish. [1. Shadows—Poetry.
2. Scottish poetry]. I. Rand, Ted, ill. II. Title.
PR5489.S5 1990 821′.8 89-24265
ISBN 0-399-22216-2
10 9 8 7 6 5 4 3 2 1
First impression

To our granddaughter Sierra Jean Schaller

I have a little shadow that goes in and out with me,
And what can be the use of him is more than I can see.

He is very, very like me from the heels up to the head;

And I see him jump before me, when I jump into my bed.

The funniest thing about him is the way he likes to grow—

Not at all like proper children, which is always very slow;

For he sometimes shoots up taller like an india-rubber ball,

And he sometimes gets so little that there's none of him at all.

He hasn't got a notion of how children ought to play,

And can only make a fool of me in every sort of way.

He stays so close beside me, he's a coward you can see;

I'd think shame to stick to nursie as that shadow sticks to me!

One morning, very early, before the sun was up,
I rose and found the shining dew on every buttercup;

But my lazy little shadow, like an arrant sleepy-head,
Had stayed at home behind me and was fast asleep in bed.